Christmas Is For Celebrating

Christmas Is For Celebrating

Melvin E. Wheatley, Jr.

THE UPPER ROOM

The Upper Room

CHRISTMAS IS FOR CELEBRATING

©1977 by The Upper Room—All rights reserved. Printed in the United States of America. No part of this book may be used or reproduced in any manner whatsoever without permission except in the case of brief quotations embodied in critical articles or reviews. For information address The Upper Room, 1908 Grand Avenue, Nashville, Tennessee 37203.

UR-366-10-0877

Unless otherwise identified, all scripture quotations are from the Revised Standard Version of the Bible, copyrighted 1946, 1952 and © 1971 by the Division of Christian Education, National Council of the Churches of Christ in the United States of America and are used by permission.

The two stanzas from the poem "Christmas Faith," Copyright 1977 by Christopher Fry, are used by permission of the author's agent Actac (Theatrical & Cinematic) Limited, 16 Cadogan Lane, London, SW1. England.

"A Tiny Egg" is from pp. 209-210 in *More Children's Worship in the Church School* by Jeanette Perkins Brown. Copyright 1953 by Harper & Row Publishers, Inc. Reprinted by the permission of the publisher.

The passage from *The Velveteen Rabbit* by Margery Williams is used by permission of Doubleday.

A word of thanks . . .

The publication of this volume is for me a form of celebrating. I feel joyfully grateful, therefore, to four people in particular who have helped it happen:

> Maxie Dunnam who affirmatively encouraged its beginnings, and Janice Grana who effectively managed its production.
>
> Betty Hauschulz who patiently typed and re-typed its pages, and Lucile Wheatley who perceptively improved and corrected its copy.

MELVIN E. WHEATLEY, JR.
Advent, 1977

CONTENTS

Foreword 11
1 The Recovery of Celebration 15
2 The Physical That Is Spiritual 23
3 The Blessedness of Receiving 35
4 The Holy That Is Here 51
5 The Divine That Is Human 67
6 The Star We Never Saw Before 79
Notes 91

FOREWORD

Great storytellers and great preachers have this in common: they find us where we are and lift us to where we might be. Melvin Wheatley does this magnificently in this book.

The celebrations of Christmas are endlessly evocative of the heart of the Christian gospel. That is why the various traditions surrounding the event of our Lord's birth are at once so terrifying and so tender. It has always seemed sad to me that some folk rationalize Christmas out of their religious sensitivity because of scholarly prejudice ("the story is not found in the earliest documents") or dogmatic consistency ("it is a vestige of a pagan festival"). The fact is that God is able to use untidiness and inconsistency in the tradition to manifest the power and the glory of the Incarnation. The first Christians were overwhelmed by the Resurrection events, and it was later that the birth stories began to stimulate imagination and faith.

Different periods of church history have seen various celebrations as central and powerful. Easter, Pentecost, All Saints' Day, and Christmas—all important and faithful celebrations of the gospel, but Christmas is the holiday most understandable and open to our time.

That is why Melvin Wheatley's reflections are so helpful. He has the capacity to sense the presence of meaning and power in the ordinary events of our days. These chapters reveal that sensitivity as he leads the reader through the "physical" and the "here" and the "human" that are infused at Christmas with the spiritual and the holy and the divine. So his writing is "incarnational." God's way with us is made visible and concrete in the places where we live and work and worry and hope.

For years at Westwood United Methodist Church in Los Angeles, the bishop preached to a congregation of university people. Preaching for him was "incarnational" in that great church. The words are made concrete and personal in his writing as well as his preaching, and that is a profound analog to the claim of the New Testament that the Word becomes flesh (John 1:14). That is the whole point of Christian existence, Christian spiritually, and Christian writing. Because the events of memory and affection are

FOREWORD

so dear to all of us in the Christmas season, we are prepared for some transcendence and joy. But the celebrations of Christmas, as Wheatley reminds us, will always be grounded in the debris of our disappointments and the flatness of our normal expectations of life.

Join me, then, in this celebration of Christmas with Bishop Wheatley and read with expectation, which is also an important part of the Christmas story.

F. Thomas Trotter

General Secretary,
The Board of Higher Education
and Ministry, The United
Methodist Church

1
THE RECOVERY OF CELEBRATION

Christmas is a season of celebration. Though we may not be aware of it, celebration is one thing many of us lack in our lives. We tend to assume that to be entertained is the same as to celebrate. They are really quite different.

To be entertained is to be acted upon by others who perform for us.
To celebrate is to act out our own performance for ourselves.

To be entertained is to have someone else help us feel good by distracting us from life as it really is.
To celebrate is to market our own affirmation of the goodness of life as it really is even with all its distractions.

CHRISTMAS IS FOR CELEBRATING

*Celebration is to greet life with a shout of "Yes!"
   instead of a sigh of "Maybe";
to dance, like Zorba the Greek, out the exuberance
   of our indebtedness;
to sing out the joy of our appreciation;
to clap with the beat of one's soul;
to praise as the harvest of one's love.*

*Celebration is to bet our days on the gamble that
   life is meant
      not merely to be chewed but to be tasted;
      not merely to be sounded but to be heard;
      not merely to be touched but to be felt;
      not merely to be looked at but to be seen;
      not merely to be endured but to be enjoyed!*

A story has been told which aptly portrays the spirit of celebration. One balmy evening, a couple accompanied their eleven-year-old son and a friend of his to the city park. The couple was on foot, the boys on bicycles. Before the parents could stop them, the boys rode into an empty playground and wheeled into a fast game of follow the leader. The sudden and noisy arrival of a policeman on a motorcycle brought their activities to an abrupt halt. Unshaken, one of the lads explained to the officer what they were playing, and politely asked him if he would like to join them. The policeman, still astride his machine, considered for a moment, then cheerily said he

would love to. There followed a dreamlike scene in which the two boys earnestly pursued the officer around the fountain, under slides, between swings, and along the edge of the sandbox. The trio eventually rode up to the playground exit. The policeman saluted and roared off! That is the spirit of celebration: spontaneous openness toward life and an affirmative involvement in it.

"All very bright and bouncy," you may respond, "but try marketing that spirit of celebration." I am willing to try, not in my own name—but in the name of the follow-the-leader event called Christmas. I am even willing to try to sell that same spirit of celebration to you, or to someone dear to you, who may be fighting feelings of grief and pain, loneliness and fear, agony and anger.

It is easy to hate Christmas. Although it may be the best season for some, for many it is the worst. Most of these individuals do not even know how large a company they keep. For many, one of the worst things about Christmas is that it is a season of so much celebration! The celebration gap between the happy and the sad tends to grow wider during Advent and Christmas than at any other time of the year. As the spirits of some people soar, the spirits of others, instead of soaring, tend to diminish and to depress. When all you feel like doing is crying, it hurts deeply to be expected to laugh.

THE RECOVERY OF CELEBRATION

What is there to celebrate
in the midst of affluence, if you are poor?
in the midst of family reunions, when you are alone?
in the midst of love, when you feel rejected?

What is there to celebrate
about the sparkling eyes of children when you are trying to deal with the deep scars of your own childhood?
about angel choruses of peace on earth when you are haunted by headlines on rising military expenditures?
about preacher-talk of "goodwill on earth" when you have just lost your job?

What is there to celebrate? Maybe nothing—if the spirit of celebration is reserved only for the lighthearted and the lucky. But let us ponder another story, related by Clarence Forsberg. One day he visited a little chapel out in the Pacific Northwest. It was a frame church and had stained glass windows and a beautiful altar. As he left the church, he stopped to sign the guest register. Leafing through the pages to see if he recognized any of the names, he spied one particular entry. No name was listed, just the date and these words, "Thank you for a place to cry."

Could it be that in a world of tears having a place to cry is something to celebrate—especially when that place celebrates Christmas, and what

THE RECOVERY OF CELEBRATION

Christmas celebrates is a heritage not of undiluted happiness but of indomitable hope?

Ralph Sockman described this wide-ranging scope of experience, appropriate for celebration. The Sockmans' only son, college age, fell to his death from their Park Avenue apartment. No satisfactory explanation of the tragedy was ever reached. A number of years after the shocking loss Dr. Sockman issued his manifesto:

Speaking personally, may I say that during the last decade of my life, things have happened to me which I cannot explain, nor can I say they were all sent of God. When I read, "All things work together for good for them that love God," the only way I can understand this in my own case is after the analogy of a ship. There are parts of a ship which taken by themselves would sink. The engine would sink. The propeller would sink. But when the parts of a ship are built together they float. So with the events of my life. Some have been tragic. Some have been happy. But when they are all built together, they form a craft that floats. Aye, more, one that I believe is going someplace. And I am comforted.[1]

Thus Christmas, properly understood, can assist the recovery of celebration for us all. The recovery of celebration hangs upon the identification of its spirit. It hangs upon the enlargement of the scope of experiences to which the spirit of celebration is deemed appropriate.

CHRISTMAS IS FOR CELEBRATING

> The darkest time in the year,
> The poorest place in the town,
> Cold, and a taste of fear,
> Man and woman alone,
> What can we hope for here?
> More light than we can learn,
> More wealth than we can treasure,
> More love than we can earn,
> More peace than we can measure,
> Because one Child is born. . . .[2]

A child was born in a world as violent as ours. That child became a man who died a violent, tortured death. Yet that infant grown to adulthood, translated into a presence, still strides across the minds and into the hearts of millions as the Man with the hope. When we join him in the game of follow the leader, he teaches us what there is to celebrate:

> *Not a world that has in it nothing but good, but a world that is good, while having in it so much that is bad;*
> *Not a life that knows no darkness, but a life in which even those who walk in darkness have seen a great light;*
> *Not a God who gives us everything we want, but a God who gives us everything we have, and offers us all we need, now and forever, to grow up full-size to the dimensions of significance and satisfactions that belong to creatures who are also co-creators.*

2
THE PHYSICAL THAT IS SPIRITUAL

And the Word became flesh and dwelt among us, full of grace and truth. . . .

John 1:14

Two television commentators were paying tribute to Thanksgiving while trying to fill up the time left on their show. There is nothing wrong with that in itself. But they paid their tribute to Thanksgiving by comparing the "authentic" meanings of Thanksgiving with the "commercialized distortions" of Christmas. That kind of comparison is dirty pool. A proper comparison never sets the best of one thing over against the worst of something else. To put down Christmas is not only aggravating but reveals a shortsighted perception on the part of the observer.

When one considers the best features of the Christmas season, it can still hold its own with any holiday or holy day. The authentic meanings of the season have not been ruined, nor should they be. We still hold the power within us either

CHRISTMAS IS FOR CELEBRATING

to sort out the authentic meanings of the season from the tinsel and the tempo that offend us, or better to find these meanings in the very midst of these characteristics of our celebration. The assignment is easy if we start where we should.

Christmas is the season for celebrating the God of all seasons. It is the special time of the year for rediscovering how close God is to us at all times of the year. Herein is the central significance of our celebration. It is not that God draws closer to us at Christmas than at any other time. God can never be any nearer to us than he always is. At every moment of our existence God presses upon us; his love never lets up on us; his creative energies always support us; his call persistently and constantly confronts us. But at Christmas—for a few bright intervals—we open the doors of our awareness wide enough to realize that it is so.

Christmas denies the popular yet erroneous assumption that the physical and the spiritual realms are incompatible. It demonstrates, rather, that the season of keenest awareness of the spiritual is precisely the season in which we give the greatest emphasis to the physical. Years ago, Archbishop William Temple observed that the way to be spiritually effective is not to ignore matter, but to use it.

During the Christmas season more than at any other time of the year, we use the material aspects of existence. Rather than detracting from the

spiritual effectiveness of the holy season, these material things supplement and enhance our awareness of the ever-present God. The visible, the audible, the tangible, the palatable, the fragrant—all mingle in one grand omelet of meaning. Candles and colored lights, holly and spun glass, carols and jingle bells, incense and perfume, candy canes and plum puddings—instead of becoming obstacles to communication between God and us, these sensuous objects "dwell among us full of grace and truth."

What does God get through to us? Love. Through the physical, God communicates a regard for us that speaks much more of devotion than of duty. God was "saying it with flowers" long before Boston florist Henry Penn turned that admonition into commercial advice.

Apart from the lavishness of love, how else do you account for mountain meadows carpeted with lupine? Apart from the extravagance of affection, how else can you explain the fragrance of a rose, the tantalizing aroma of coffee in the early morning, the lingering afterglow of a sunset punctuating the day with its exclamation mark of glory?

Turning away from the sunset serenade of gorgeous colors bouncing off the Grand Canyon, a young woman said disdainfully to her companion, "It just isn't relevant!" From the practical perspective, the young lady standing on the rim

THE PHYSICAL THAT IS SPIRITUAL

of the canyon was quite correct. From a strict subsistence point of view, sunsets are not relevant. Violets are worthless, orchids are parasitical, meadowlarks are meaningless sources of sounds, and a smile is a waste of muscular energy. Only in a system of value in which the sensuously pleasurable is called good do orchids and meadowlarks and Grand Canyon sunsets make sense! God does want us not merely to endure life, but to enjoy it.

Yet we are reticent to accentuate this positive, pleasurable aspect of providence. Years ago Leslie Weatherhead asked for an explanation. He wanted to know why it is that whenever we start talking about the "will of God" in our lives, we always have in mind some tragedy, some burden, that we do not want? As a typical example he cited the lines of a once familiar hymn:

> Should pining sickness waste away
> My life in premature decay,
> My Father, still I strive to say,
> Thy will be done.

What a terrible God such a hymn supposes! I wish someone would write a hymn incorporating the idea that we should sing "Thy will be done" when we have played eighteen holes of golf on a glorious morning, or played four sets of tennis on a summer evening. We should sing "Thy will be done" as we get out of our cold bath, tingling all over with health and energy, or when we rejoice in the glories of a sunset, or when we watch our children open their stockings on Christmas morning, or sit down to dinner later on that same blessed day, or are thrilled by the glory of wonderful music or the love of a friend, or the worship of God's house.[3]

But there is more. God uses the physical as spiritual not only to communicate love, but also to instruct us in truth. God was the first teacher who made extensive use of audiovisual materials. From the beginning, God has been a multimedia enthusiast! God's sharpest pupils, consequently, have always been those who learned life's lessons from the simplest things.

Moses heard God's call to vocation through the flaming bush. The writer of Proverbs saw instruction for lazy men in the industriousness of the ants. Amos caught his image of divine justice from a builder's plumbline revealing the true angle of a wall. Hosea used the molehill of his own mercy toward his faithless wife to measure the mountain-dimension of God's forgiving love toward all his prodigal sons and daughters.

Jesus was the most apt pupil of all. The lilies of the field were instructions in trust. The unprejudiced rain falling on the just and the unjust was the wideness of God's mercy. The growth of the mustard seed was the graph of God's kingdom maturing in the human heart. A pinch of leaven in a pound of dough was the role of the moral individual in an immoral society. The absence

THE PHYSICAL THAT IS SPIRITUAL

of figs among the thistles to satisfy hunger became a demonstration of the harvest of consequence in the cultivation of character.

We, too, can learn the spiritual lessons of eternity from the tangible instruments of time. We can discover that many things that look alike are not alike at all but different. World renowned mathematician and scientific philosopher the late J. Bronowski observed,

> Simply as a biological engine, each man can distinguish sharply between his own set of proteins and the next man's. For example, if I scar my face and want to repair it, I must use for the patch a piece of skin from myself (or an identical twin self). It does not matter from what part of my body I take the skin: it will be accepted by my face as mine even if it comes from my back. But if I graft a piece of your skin on my face, it will be rejected, even if it comes from the same place on your face. My body chemicals can make another face, but not by matching faces—by matching me; and you are not me.[4]

We can learn that many things that look simple are complex. The man who talked with flowers, George Washington Carver, took one peanut, and from the ordinary peanut, learned so many of God's lessons. He made paper out of the shell, dye from the red skin, milk and butter and metal polish—and a hundred other products—from the nut itself.

We can learn, too, that many things that look

ugly in the beginning become beautiful at last. So Jeanette Perkins Brown observes:

> A tiny egg once held a germ
> That grew and grew into a worm;
> The worm grew bigger than its skin,
> And left the shell 'twas living in;
> And still it grew, until it spun
> A chrysalis. *Still life went on.*
>
> For from the chrysalis there came
> New life, but changed in form and name.
> With fluttering wings of beauty rare
> A butterfly rose in the air.
>
> *The worm it once was could not guess*
> *It ever would wear such a dress,*
> *For born within those tiny germs*
> *Is life beyond the dreams of worms.*[5]

It seems like magic, but it is not magic at all. It is God. Everywhere about us, God's spiritual truths and working principles of life wait to be understood by us through material things.

God is with us through the physical that is spiritual not only to communicate love to us and to instill truth in us, but also to transmit energies through us. We talk about working together with God. But how does God use us—really? Surely not in some nebulous fashion when we have both feet firmly planted in midair. We are most effec-

tive co-workers with God when we are translating God's grace into tangible deeds that help, and communicating God's truth into insights and actions that heal.

During World War II, when there was such an acute housing shortage all over our country, an eastern family relocated on the west coast in Stockton, California. They were forced to live for a number of months in a hotel. After a time, the young son in that family became a familiar sight around the hotel—so much so that one of the permanent residents finally felt free to say to him, "What's the matter, Sonny, don't you have any home?" "Of course we have a home. We just can't find a house to put it in!" he replied.

Christmas is the perennial reminder that God's predicament is like that. God has workable principles of peace. He is just having a hard time finding nations mature enough and a world organization effective enough to practice those principles of peace. God cares about the disadvantaged youth of the world's ghettos. He just needs more effective individuals and agencies through which to communicate that care. God has seeds of reconciliation for bitter lives tragically alienated from one another because of deep misunderstandings. He just needs more human soil of repentance and forgiveness in which to drop those seeds.

Instead, then, of wasting our time fretting about

THE PHYSICAL THAT IS SPIRITUAL

the many things that most assuredly can be wrong with Christmas, let us celebrate the tangibles associated with the season that are still very right. As we use the material rather than ignore it, not only will the heavens continue to declare God's glory, but also the physical about us will become a source of spiritual renewal within us:

> *Our food will be flavored with God's love;*
> *Our candles will flicker with God's truth;*
> *Our houses, as well as our hearts, will become*
>   *God's home.*

3

THE BLESSEDNESS OF RECEIVING

And Mary said, "My soul magnifies the Lord, and my spirit rejoices in God my Savior. . . ."

Luke 1:46-47

One of the best celebrations of Christmas is receiving. No, my pen did not slip. I did not mean *giving*. I meant *receiving*. We pay too little tribute to the blessedness of receiving. We hear that it is "more blessed to give than to receive" so often that we tend to distort this truth into a falsehood. We begin to feel as though life is a matter of giving *or* receiving and that giving is good and receiving is bad. As a matter of reality, life is a process of giving *and* receiving. Indeed, a healthy attitude toward receiving makes giving possible. Receiving and giving complement each other; without one, the other suffers.

Personal counselors are familiar with the practical consequences of the failure to accept this. It is reflected in the deep discomfort that so many of us feel whenever we give any honest, open thought to ourselves. As long as we are

THE BLESSEDNESS OF RECEIVING

doing things for others we feel virtuous and comfortable. The minute we begin, as we put it, "to think of ourselves," we feel guilty and selfish. This attitude assumes that other human beings have legitimate needs and desires that deserve to be satisfied, while our needs must be imaginary and our desires unreasonable. The opposite assumption seems more nearly justified. If other people may rightfully receive from us, then we may rightfully expect to receive from other people. And that is what makes Christmas so wonderful! It is the season in which we do receive so much from so many.

Christmas meets our elemental need to be noticed. Back in the more prosperous days of the British Empire, a London slum-dweller complained, "What does it profit a man to be a citizen of an Empire on which the sun never sets, if he lives in an alley on which the sun never rises?" That is more than a complaint against slums. It is a statement of fact. Deep down inside every human being is the need and the right to claim his or her own place in the sun.

So deep is this need that unless we can satisfy it in healthy ways, we go about satisfying it in sick ways—from temper tantrums to malingering illnesses, from headline-grabbing to name-dropping, from chronic pouting to compulsive shoplifting, from grandstanding at the country club to drag racing on city streets. What devices

CHRISTMAS IS FOR CELEBRATING

we human beings do come up with to call attention to ourselves! Why? The need to be noticed cries out in us just that boisterously. Until we are noticed we are naughted, and we would rather be naughty than be naughted! We would rather be a pain in somebody's neck than a cipher in everybody's mind.

Let's not let this temptation to satisfy this need in distorted ways trap us into the notion that the need for attention is itself a sign of sickness. It is not. It is much more accurately a sign of the social aspect of our selfhood. My capacity to consider myself a worthy entity is inescapably related to the willingness and the readiness of other persons in my experience to acknowledge my existence as significant. The feelings I have about myself are indelibly stained by the color of the feelings of others about me and communicated to me. Though in this we may vary in degree, all of us are similar in kind. The loneliness of life is never more frightening than in those dark moments of the soul when we are fogged in by the feeling that nobody really cares.

At four years of age I had that experience common to almost every child. I got lost. As a country boy from the dirt streets of Ridgely, Maryland, with its eleven hundred proud citizens, I visited my grandmother in Philadelphia. For a big treat she took me to Gimbel Brothers, then to Wanamaker's department store to show me

THE BLESSEDNESS OF RECEIVING

the sights. Our stories never did agree as to who wandered off from whom. All I know for sure is that suddenly Grandmother was not there. She was nowhere to be seen. It was no use to call out to her because she was deaf. There was no arguing the fact that I was lost. Although I was surrounded by great numbers of people, none of them knew me or noticed me. For moments that seemed like years, I suffered the terrible panic which is so much a part of the predicament of feeling lost. I continued to exist in space and time, but my existence was turned into a nightmare because no one else seemed to know about it or to be concerned with it. Only when Grandmother turned the corner and gave me her smile of recognition did my existence turn into a reason for joy!

But some of the best as well as the worst experiences come out of this vital need to be noticed. One summer, a number of years ago, one of our sons came running into the house with a smile a mile wide. His whole being shouted the news that something tremendously important had just happened. And it had. His second-grade teacher of the year before had just driven past the house and waved to him!

John F. Kennedy was a master of the art of noticing. He had a somewhat boyish friendliness which was characteristic of his public image as well as when there were no crowds. He did not allow differences of political opinions to affect his personal friendship. Kennedy had an ability to spot the faces of his friends and would go out of his way to speak to them or wave his hand or maybe just nod to them. And he would always have something really personal to say. A newspaper columnist told the following story. Kennedy once walked fifty yards out of his way crossing the White House lawn to come over to say to the columnist, "Hey, did you see our picture in the paper?" Apparently the columnist had happened to be standing close by when Kennedy signed an autograph for an admirer, and they had both appeared in a photo in that day's newspaper.

One of the priceless gifts bestowed by Christmas is that it doesn't happen the rest of the year. At this special time life walks fifty yards across the lawn and calls us by name. Whether we are newspaper boys or milkmen, garbage collectors or distant relatives, old friends or new colleagues, we are not left standing alone and lost in the complex maze of modern existence. Cards or gifts, cheery greetings or party invitations with our names on them seek us out to feed our need to be noticed.

Our abundant receiving of this season is blessed for another reason. There is a growing body of evidence to suggest that we never outgrow our dependence on others. What begins as

a physical requirement for human survival persists as an emotional and spiritual necessity for human significance. In innumerable ways Christmas meets and ministers to our need to be nurtured, our need to draw all kinds of sustenance from other persons, not just their attention. There are infantile expressions of this need, such things as compulsive dependency, parasitical possessiveness, a "star-boarder" complex. But let's not let these distortions of truth trap us into missing the truth itself.

The negative tribute to our need for nurture can be read from some of the most common denominators of our daily existence: our vulnerability to criticism; our sense of loneliness when misunderstood; our feeling of frustration when we cannot seem to get through to someone about whom we care; the spiritual and intellectual malnutrition which sets in when for too long we separate ourselves from stimulating and inspiring people.

The positive tributes to this truth are quite as common and unmistakable: the warm feeling of well-being when we are in love; the sense of security which flows in with almost measurable force when we have encountered someone who really does seem to understand; the glow which irradiates our being when we are accorded even the simplest kindness; the reinforcement we gather to go on after exposure to someone who

THE BLESSEDNESS OF RECEIVING

courageously follows whatever light he or she has in glad adventuring for more light.

Christmas generously and variously meets our nurture needs. Even the commercial realm functions in this fashion at times. Several years ago I picked up a copy of the *San Francisco Chronicle* and caught one of Herb Caen's columns. That particular day he was telling about Jim Ludwig, then general manager of Sak's Fifth Avenue branch store in San Francisco. Jim had just received a letter a few days earlier which had in it a ten-dollar money order from a Mrs. Anna Barber, who lived in the East. She said she was a widow, seventy-five years old and living alone. She did not expect to receive any gifts that Christmas. She requested that someone pick out ten dollars worth of things and send them to her. It did not matter what was sent; she was simply looking forward to receiving a surprise package from San Francisco.

There was a footnote to Herb Caen's story. Jim Ludwig not only complied with the original request. He sent a copy of the letter to Sak's main office in New York City, where it filtered down the chain of command. On Christmas of that year, Mrs. Anna Barber received ten dollars worth of gifts not just from Sak's in San Francisco, but from every Sak's Fifth Avenue across the country—all nineteen branches. I am not suggesting that you write that kind of letter, but it is

THE BLESSEDNESS OF RECEIVING

encouraging that such a letter once elicited that response!

This nurturing spirit of the season gets through to our children, too. A friend told me about an eight-year-old nephew of hers who was called upon for a part in the children's presentation of the nativity scene. Much to his distress, he was assigned the role of the innkeeper who had to turn Joseph and Mary away from the inn when they arrived. He suffered mightily over the necessity of making such a harsh speech. When the time came for the pageant and Joseph and Mary came up to the door of the inn, the boyish "innkeeper" bravely carried through with his assigned line—with a slight addition. Responding to their request for room, he said: "I'm sorry, there is no room in the inn . . . but wouldn't you like to come in for a cup of coffee?"

At the level of personal encounter at Christmas, many of us are thus nurtured. Every gift received is a care package expressing concern for our well-being. Every card with our name upon it is a line of communication being restrung or maintained. Every impressive nativity portrayal is a visual aid for our inspiration. Every musical presentation can become a representation of that first angel chorus.

There is a final reason this season of receiving is so blessed. Christmas showers us with the treasures that not only meet our need to be noticed, and supply our need to be nurtured, but also enable us to fulfill our need to be needed. To the degree that we freely receive, and only to that degree are we able freely to give. Whether the content of the exchange be inspiration or wisdom, love or money, we are able to share only that which we do possess. And to a marked degree, we are able to possess only that which others have first shared with us.

This is as true of the greatest as of the humblest. Most of us are reasonably certain that if we are ever to be even tin-haloed saints, we are going to need to have considerable inspiration and guidance from other people. Often we assume that there are those for whom this is not the case. We may feel that some lucky people arrive in life with built-in inspiration and automated guidance. This is not true.

A delightful episode from Albert Schweitzer's life argues otherwise. A number of years ago on his way to Aspen, Colorado, Schweitzer changed trains in Chicago. As he was standing on the station platform being questioned by reporters, a woman carrying a heavy suitcase walked past. Immediately Dr. Schweitzer excused himself. He walked over to the lady, took the heavy suitcase from her, and accompanied her to the car of the train she was boarding. Then he turned and walked back to where the clustered group had been. They were no longer there. Each one of

THE BLESSEDNESS OF RECEIVING

the reporters, seeing Albert Schweitzer's helpfulness, had started to look for some lady with a heavy suitcase to assist onto the train!

Forty years before the Chicago episode, Dr. Schweitzer and his wife were being moved from one prisoner-of-war camp to another. He reported in his autobiography:

> At the station at Tarascon we had to wait for the arrival of our train in a distant goods-shed. My wife and I, heavily laden with baggage, could hardly get along . . . between the lines. Thereupon a poor cripple whom I had treated in the camp came forward to help us. He had no baggage because he possessed nothing, and I was much moved by his offer, which I accepted. While we walked along side by side in the scorching sun, I vowed to myself that in memory of him I would in the future always keep a lookout at stations for heavily laden people, and help them. And this vow I have kept. On one occasion, however, my offer made me suspected of thievish intentions![6]

The point of the two stories in the Christmas context is not that Dr. Schweitzer inspired generous behavior in others, but rather that "this man for others" acknowledged that precisely this form of helpfulness was inspired in him *by* others.

Schweitzer's story is a parable of Christmas. The human dimensions of this season, as we authentically celebrate it, are actually our responses to the divine dimensions as they have come down to us from the beginning. Mary's words in the Magnificat sing it beautifully:

My soul magnifies the Lord, and my spirit rejoices in God my Savior.
He has regarded the low estate of his handmaiden . . . . [God noticed me!]
He who is mighty has done great things for me. [God nurtured me!]
He exalted those of low degree. [God needs me!]
Luke 1:46-52

So it is, now as then, Christmas turns our faces toward the hope side of history reminding us of the blessedness of our receiving.

> *In the gift of Jesus, God notices us. We are neither out of sight nor out of mind. We are eternally and intimately the objects of attention and affection.*
>
> *In the gift of Jesus, God nourishes us. God instructs us with truth; and sustains us with presence.*
>
> *And just as surely, in the gift of Jesus, we are served notice that God needs us. The same spirit that dwelt in Jesus is meant to come and dwell in us. That same quality of love that enabled him to become "a man for others" is meant to set us to caring, too.*

Of course, it is blessed to give. But giving is not all that is blessed. Receiving is blessed, too.

THE BLESSEDNESS OF RECEIVING

Because it is the receiving that makes the giving possible. Joyously affirming all that Christmas has brought, and does bring to us—let *our* souls magnify the Lord, and let our spirits rejoice in God, our Savior!

4

THE HOLY THAT IS HERE

And this will be a sign for you: you will find a babe wrapped in swaddling cloths and lying in a manger.

Luke 2:12

One morning, sitting by my window working, I sensed the presence of God. It was nothing I did. It was something I saw. A Japanese gardener, ancient in appearance yet spry in actions, was busy about his chores in the yard next door. His truck was parked in my line of vision in such a way that every time he returned to it for a tool, he caught my eye. When I could not see him, I could hear his mechanical mower and the rhythmic biting of his shears.

Quite accustomed to the noise, I became aware after a while that all had become quiet. Looking up I saw the gardener in the cab of his truck. He was eating lunch. But he was not eating all of it. Three blue jays were sharing it with him. They were not stealing it. They were invited guests. One at a time each bird would light on the windowsill of his truck. Expecting the bird,

THE HOLY THAT IS HERE

the gardener would break off a piece of his sandwich and hold it out. Taking it from his hand the blue jay would fly with it to a nearby branch. Then another bird would take a turn. This went on as long as lunch lasted. When the lunch was gone, the gardener rolled up the window.

There was something simple and yet authentic about the scene. I determined to check another day. Sure enough, every Saturday at noon the ritual was repeated. It became for me a sort of sacramental meal, at which I saw a gardener sharing his bread with birds, but in which I sensed the presence of the living God.

At first it struck me as strange that so simple a scene should hit me with such force. But then I remembered Moses and the flaming bush. More than that, I remembered the manger in Bethlehem which is at the center of the Christmas celebration. Then it began to seem strange that I should be so surprised. Of all of the messages God seems to have been trying to get through to us across the centuries, none has been repeated more often I would guess than this: the God of Moses and the God of the manger can be counted on to be forever appearing in the most unlikely places. God's daily word to us is, "Don't wear out your shoes running off to some other place seeking that which is holy. 'Put off your shoes for the place where you are now standing is holy ground.' "

CHRISTMAS IS FOR CELEBRATING

We are not fully convinced of this, of course. To us it is one of the oddities of Advent that Jesus was born in the crude accomodations of a side-street stable. Impressed as we are with pretentious externals and status symbols, this simplicity bothers us. So we look for someone to blame. We look so hard, in fact, that we conjure up an image of a hard-bitten innkeeper who selfishly turned aside a poor couple he could have assisted. But nowhere in the New Testament will you encounter such a character. He simply does not exist in any gospel account of the first Christmas. The manger was called into use in Luke's nativity narrative for a simple reason plainly stated, "There was no room in the inn."

If the birth of Jesus in a manger is not an unfortunate mistake occasioned by the perverse nature of man, then how are we to view it? As a delightfully appropriate revelation of the essential nature of God! The point of the manger is not that if we were more *receptive* we would make room for God in our royal suites. The point of the manger is that if we were more *perceptive* we would remain ready to recognize and receive God at whatever unlikely places he appears. When we believe in God, we can know there will be many surprises.

One of those surpises is that the God revealed to us in Christmas feels very much at home at a humble address. We may not, but God does.

THE HOLY THAT IS HERE

God confounds us by appearing from modest accomodations. If the Christmas story teaches us nothing else it should remind us unmistakably that nobody is anybody because of the section of the city where he or she is born. Over and over again in this world God has a way of planting majesty in a manger and luring the highest qualities from the humblest quarters.

Biography is an incarnation of this contention. Abraham Lincoln is now recognized as perhaps the man of greatest moral stature the nineteenth century produced. Yet his greatness was garbed in such humility that most of his contemporaries missed it. Almost daily the press carried intemperate attacks upon Lincoln's intelligence, his appearance, his character. As late as June 9, 1864, less than a year before his assassination, the *New York World* published this paragraph: "The age of statesmen is gone, the age of rail-splitters and tailors, of buffoons, boors, and fanatics, has succeeded. In a crisis of almost appalling magnitude, the country is asked to consider the claims of two ignorant, boorish, third-rate, backwoods lawyers for the highest station in the government. God save the Republic." God did exactly that! He saved the republic with the help of one of those backwoods lawyers!

There is another surprise to be found in the manger. The God that Christmas reveals to us feels very much at home not only at a humble

THE HOLY THAT IS HERE

address but also in a secular, which is to say in a "non-religious," setting. This we forget too easily.

If I had not already known the nativity story when I first visited Bethlehem, I would have come away convinced that Jesus was born neither in an inn nor in a stable but in an ornate church. That is the way subsequent generations have made it appear. Even as I walked through the church that covers the spot on which Jesus is traditionally presumed to have been born, there was crowded from my mind any image that I might have had of a manger setting such as we see portrayed every year on cards or with nativity figures. It was crowded out by innumerable votive lights and ecclesiastical trappings that everywhere surrounded me. It was almost as if those early churchmen could not accept the idea that God could feel at home anywhere, not just in a church sanctuary. And so, stuck with an embarrassing bit of Christian biography, they built a church over the manger to hide the truth. The understandable tendency to erect a "sacred" shrine over the "secular" spot where a notable happening occurred is thus turned into the regrettable assumption that a "sacred" shrine is the likeliest spot for a notable happening to occur.

That narrow kind of ecclesiasticism can crowd the living God out of life as fast as crass commercialism. Perhaps one of the least inspiring dramas

CHRISTMAS IS FOR CELEBRATING

in the world is the self-concious "religious" drama, plays that set out to be pious and end up being insipid. For that matter is there anything less inspiring in this world than a self-consciously "religious" prayer, a prayer that presumes that God must always be addressed in a sepulchral tone dripping in sugary sentimentalities? A United Methodist bishop heard a prayer like that. Immediately he turned to a ministerial friend and asked him what he thought of the prayer. The friend replied, "Well, if you ask me, Bishop, God had to reach for the Alka Seltzer after that one!"

It is really no laughing matter. This compartmentalized concept of God and this anemic notion of religion will never meet the needs of our time. But the God of the manger can and does. The God of Christmas is a this-worldly God:

> *Who meets us in a baby's low cry as well as in the vastness of the universe;*
> *Who is just as much at home in the acrid odors of the stable as in the incensed atmosphere of the sanctuary;*
> *Who is with us in the sweat hours of toil as well as in the sweet hour of prayer;*
> *Who uses our "secular" activities quite as much as our sacred liturgies to accomplish holy intentions.*

The late Wallace Hamilton delightfully and

THE HOLY THAT IS HERE

disarmingly illustrated this point in terms of our dreams of one world of peace. Though we are still far from the realization of our dreams, to the degree that we are drawing close to them at all, Hamilton suggested that credit is due to people whom we normally would not even acknowledge.

> Certainly no one has contributed more to the physical oneness of mankind than the builders of railroads, steamships, and jet planes—or the inventors of telephones, television, Telstar, and all these wonderful tele-things. They have succeeded far more than theologians or philosophers in making humanity one—not that they intended to do it or had the faintest notion that they were.[7]

A God who feels at home in a secular as well as a sacred setting uses craftsmen who are not even aware of the full implications of what they are doing to help move the world in the direction of divine purposes.

The God who planted majesty in a manger has another surprise for us in that place. The God of Christmas feels at home not only at a humble address, and in a secular setting, but also in the most ordinary details of daily routine. This we are inclined to forget because we have covered the nativity story with so much poetry that it is hard to get down to the prose of the situation.

We have a saying that the only sure things in life are death and taxes. We know, of course, that one other thing has to be sure if these other two are to follow—and that is birth. So it is that rather than concentrating on the exceptional experiences of life, the nativity narrative actually features two of the most universal experiences of the human family, birth and taxes. An old familiar plot is being developed—a husband and wife becoming a father and a mother. And how do they happen to be where they are? In Bethlehem celebrating some high holy days, or some great national festival? Not at all. They are there for the very common and painful business of registering to pay their taxes!

Now further strip the poetry away from the prose. Matthew's wonderful tradition shows the Wise Men bringing gold, frankincense, and myrrh. But who came bringing bread, milk, and honey? The songs and stories in Luke present the shepherds bowing down before them. But who came in to help tidy up for them? Who got supper? Did Joseph? Or did he hold the baby while Mary prepared the meal?

All this is to say what should be more obvious than it is. The daily routine of the holy family was much more like our own routine than we are inclined to picture it. Yet so much of the time we assume that if we could only change the routine of our days into more exciting patterns God would be with us. The message of the manger is exactly the opposite of that! If we only

THE HOLY THAT IS HERE

open our awareness to God's presence with us, that will change the routine of our days into a much more exciting pattern. Archbishop Temple said that the spiritually minded person differs from the materially minded person not in that he deals with different things but in that he deals with the same things differently.[8]

I think we particularly need to see this in relation to forms of Christmas celebrating. Of course, people are inclined to become too busy and exhausted cooking and shopping, writing cards and decorating homes, participating in worship services and joining with friends in parties and with families in reunions. But what is the alternative to this type of hustle and busyness?

Cynics with a Scrooge mentality toward Christmas would say, "Give it all up. Eliminate all this routine." Give up those mince pies? Forget those friends? Restrain that impulse to be extra generous for one month in twelve? Tell those country cousins to stay home where they belong? Rule out such sentimental symbols as Christmas trees and candlelight? Forget the nonsense about a Christmas eve service? After giving up all these traditions, then what? Then, with all the time thus saved, we can set out to capture the *true* spirit of the season? Well, all right. But how? How capture the true spirit of the season?

A lady once asked that question early in Advent. With her husband she was looking for an

THE HOLY THAT IS HERE

appropriate Christmas card. She found one she liked with a little sprig of holly in the corner and great big letters spelling L O V E, covering the front of the card. Turning to her husband she wondered whether it was "Christmassy" enough.

That is a good question. But how do you make love and generosity "Christmassy" enough except by living them? How do you live them except in relationships? What are relationships made of except cooking and shopping, writing cards and decorating homes, participating in worship services and sharing with those who need, visiting with families and gathering with friends? What we need to do is not to eliminate the routine but to illuminate it. What we need is not to change all that we are doing so that we can find God, but to let God find us through what we are doing so that will change everything.

This chapter began with God finding me one Saturday morning through a Japanese gardener sharing his lunch with three blue jays. God also found me one day through a conversation I overheard between a horse talking to a rabbit. I did not exactly overhear the conversation. I read the report of one who did. The source of the conversation was Margery Williams' story about a velveteen rabbit received by a little boy as a Christmas present.

CHRISTMAS IS FOR CELEBRATING

Nursery magic is very strange and wonderful, and only those playthings that are old and wise and experienced like the Skin Horse understand all about it.

"What is REAL?" asked the Rabbit one day, when they were lying side by side near the nursery fender, before Nana came to tidy the room. "Does it mean having things that buzz inside you and a stick-out handle?"

"Real isn't how you are made," said the Skin Horse. "It's a thing that happens to you. When a child loves you for a long, long time, not just to play with, but REALLY loves you, then you become Real."

"Does it hurt?" asked the Rabbit.

"Sometimes," said the Skin Horse, for he was always truthful. "When you are Real you don't mind being hurt."

"Does it happen all at once, like being wound up," he asked, "or bit by bit?"

"It doesn't happen all at once," said the Skin Horse. "You become. It takes a long time. That's why it doesn't often happen to people who break easily, or have sharp edges, or who have to be carefully kept. Generally, by the time you are Real, most of your hair has been loved off, and your eyes drop out and you get loose in the joints and very shabby. But these things don't matter at all, because once you are Real you can't be ugly, except to people who don't understand." [9]

Well, celebrants of Christmas become people who do understand. They understand that they are real and everybody is real because Somebody called God has loved them into being Real. Such is the message of the Christmas manger. It keeps telling us about a God who is forever luring the

THE HOLY THAT IS HERE

highest qualities from the humblest quarters, turning secular settings into holy ground, and making ordinary tasks flame with a special meaning.

As surely as you and I celebrate Christmas by preparing our lives for that kind of God to come into our midst, we shall make our own amazing discovery. The Holy is already here!

5

THE DIVINE THAT IS HUMAN

The Christ you have to deal with is not a weak person outside you, but a tremendous power inside you.
2 Corinthians 13:3 (PHILLIPS)

Some people have been greatly disturbed lest we lose Christ out of Christmas. I am concerned lest we lose Christ *in* Christmas. Some are afraid that we will not talk enough about a baby born in a Bethlehem stable. I fear that we shall talk about that baby in such a way as to make him wholly irrelevant to babies born in modern hospitals. They fear that we shall neglect the good news that God was in Jesus. I fear that we shall neglect the momentous meaning of that news—God is in us.

There is little reason to suppose that we shall ever neglect the annual pageantry of the Christmas season. But we may miss the intimate implications of the pageant. We shall keep Christ in Christmas all right, but we shall keep him there as a first-century oddity rather than as a twentieth-century reality. We shall find him in the manger, but lose him in the market. We shall recognize him wrapped in swaddling cloths, but not detect him dressed in jeans. We shall indentify the Christ spirit in the life of Jesus, but fail utterly to comprehend that the Christ spirit may be living on our street.

As something of a corrective, therefore, let us consider the words of the man who wrote closest in time to the actual life of Jesus, as translated by a man who talks a language closest to our own. According to the apostle Paul as translated by J. B. Phillips: "The Christ you have to deal with is not a weak person outside you, but a tremendous power inside you." Christmas is for celebrating that—the Christ with which we have to deal.

But such celebrating raises a question. What do we mean by "Christ in or out of Christmas"? If we are to keep Christ, anytime, we need to be clearer than we are on what we mean. There is no area of our religious thinking more confused than this. I am not talking about our hair-splitting theological disagreements with one another. I am talking, rather, about our being so consistently inconsistent with ourselves. In one breath we speak of Christ when we mean the historical person Jesus. In the next breath we use precisely the same word to describe the spiritual quality of life toward which we aspire. On the one hand

THE DIVINE THAT IS HUMAN

we call ourselves sinful because we are not Christlike. We then turn around and consider ourselves presumptuous for thinking we could be.

If you would feel how raw the edges of our confusion really are, take these lines of one of our favorite carols:

> O holy Child of Bethlehem,
> Descend on us, we pray;
> Cast out our sin, and enter in,
> Be born in us today.[10]

Granted that stanza is a lovely sentiment, what sense does it really make? When you translate the poetry into prose, when you say it instead of sing it, what does it mean? Are we actually asking that a real baby who was born nineteen centuries ago should somehow be born in us today? Of course we mean nothing so crude as that. Then what do we mean? In what manner that makes any sense can the Christ with which the first-century Christmas began be the Christ with which the twentieth-century Christmas continues? In what way is the Christ with which Jesus had to deal related to the Christ with which you and I have to deal?

There have been libraries of books written in scholarly attempts to answer this question to the satisfaction of all. No one attempt has ever succeeded. But consider this working answer to this question which is at the heart of the Christmas celebration.

The Christ with which Jesus had to deal can be the Christ with which we have to deal, provided that by *Christ* we mean at least three things:

1. Something that is spiritual, not physical, but something spiritual that is compatible with the physical though not restricted by it.
2. Something that is eternal not temporal, but something eternal that is compatible with the temporal though not restricted by it.
3. Something universal, not individual or unique, but something universal that is compatible with the individual or unique though not restricted by it.

Christ then is the spiritual, eternal, universal, quality of life which is compatible with but not restricted to the physical, temporal, individual unit which we think of as a human being. Christ equals the divine quality of life which God places within human capacity.

Phillips Brooks, who wrote the lines about the holy child of Bethlehem descending upon us and entering into us, apparently had this understanding. He also wrote the lines:

> The feet of the humblest may walk in the field
> Where the feet of the holiest trod,
> This, then, is the marvel revealed to mortals

THE DIVINE THAT IS HUMAN

When the silvery trumpets of Christmas have pealed,
That mankind are the children of God.[11]

But if God is the source of this Christ potential and everything we read in our Scriptures nourishes that presupposition and if all God's children are its recipients, then why do we need Christmas? What does Christmas have to do with the universal Christ with which we have to deal?

Christmas celebrates the birth of one boy child, who lived at one time, in one place and one body. That boy child's name was Jesus. Through the centuries Christians have learned to speak of the boy child matured into a man as Jesus Christ. But what we Christians usually forget, when we use that phrase that is so familiar to us, is that in referring to Jesus as Jesus Christ, we are making a value judgment which the majority of the human family does not share with us. For when we call the man Jesus Christ, we are pointing to that one precise human being in history and saying, "There is God's personification of the quality of life which God is eager and willing to share with human beings when human beings are ready and willing to share with God."

To put it in a modern idiom, Jesus, for Christians, is "Mr. Christ." We understand that way of saying things. For example, if I should tell you that in Stockton, California, our family lived across the street from "Mr. Football," whom would you name as our neighbor? The more you know about football history, the more likley you would be to guess correctly that we lived across the street from Amos Alonzo Stagg. You would know that in the minds of students of the game, coaches, sports writers, and fans, A. A. Stagg was "Mr. Football." That is to say, he was the personification of the most and best values to be found in that game. So, for Christians, as far as the game of life is meant to be lived and played by human beings, Jesus is "Mr. Life."

Or use another idiom with which we are familiar. Magazine ads offer us "Heifetz in Hi-fidelity." What's the point? In hi-fidelity, the surface noise of the medium is so nearly eliminated and that which is reproduced is so natural, the experience of listening to the recording is very close to the experience of sitting in the concert hall and listening to the artist in person.

So, Jesus is the truth of God about the Creator and about God's creatures recorded in the highest fidelity possible on a human instrument. He is God's symphony of love played with minimum interference from the surface noise of the self through which it was being played. After nineteen hundred years we are convinced as we listen that the music is played precisely as the composer wanted it to be played. In that sense it is the music of the composer as well as of the performer.

As such a hi-fidelity recording of the Christ

THE DIVINE THAT IS HUMAN

quality of life, Jesus is unique. Not in the sense that he has a corner on such quality. It is precisely the Christ quality of Jesus that makes him universal, not unique—like us, not different from us. But Jesus is unique in that he is one human being of whom God has been able to make all that God wanted to make. Jesus is one human being who has been entirely willing to let God enable him. Harold DeWolf writes,

God may, for all we know, have called others before Jesus, others who faltered and failed to fulfill the high hard vocation to which God called them. Though Jesus faltered, he did not fail.[12]

The supreme capacity and vocation with which Jesus was endowed by God were the capacity and vocation which he fully dedicated to God.

This brings us now to the baffling question about our relationship to this Jesus. Did he succeed perfectly to live out the tremendous power which was the Christ with which he had to deal because God made it impossible for him to fail? If so, then his success has no relevance to our efforts. Surely it takes no clinical analysis to uncover the fact that God has given us no such goodness by automation. But if Jesus' faithful stewardship was not automatic, what is the explanation? The only answer which makes any sense to me is to say that Jesus was faithful because he chose to be as faithful as he was capable of being.

In this, he is both our problem and our promise. He is our problem because he consistently chose the way we so inconsistently choose. He haunts us with the reminder of how much more God might have forgiven, taught, loved through us in days that are now no more. If only we had chosen to be as loving and as truthful, as compassionate and as just, as we know we could have chosen to be, but did not so choose! The surface static of the selves through which God was trying to communicate love and truth, compassion and justice was too loud with our self-centeredness.

At the same time Jesus is our promise. He haunts us with the reminder of the Christ quality of life which God implants potentially within each soul. "The light which lightens everyone coming into the world" can still become dominant in our lives, too. In the light of his life, though we know that we may not become all that he was and is, we know just as surely that we can become much more than we have been and are.

Here is a simple illustration. Every year at Christmas I get out my trumpet. I may not have played it at all during the other eleven and a half months, but when the Christmas carols start ringing, I get the urge to loosen up those valves and start playing. That seasonal fact always brings to mind one of our favorite family stories. During

CHRISTMAS IS FOR CELEBRATING

our Stockton days Raphael Mendez used to come to the University of Pacific with his twin sons to perform and to instruct in the Summer Music Camp. For our family Raphael Mendez has ever since been "Mr. Trumpet." But apparently my son's enthusiasm for Raphael Mendez was based, in part, on his lack of enthusiasm for my trumpet playing. On one occasion, after hearing Mendez play, that son handed down his verdict: "Gee, Mom, if Dad practiced a thousand years he'd never sound like that, would he?" And he was so right. But if Dad practiced a thousand years, really disciplined himself enough to practice, he would come much closer to sounding like that than he has ever yet come!

So, if we practice living out the supreme potential in us a thousand years, we shall never reproduce Jesus. Our capacity is not his capacity. But we do not have to go back twenty centuries to discover that we vary in capacities. Our vocation is not his vocation. And we do not have to go back two thousand years to find that our vocations differ. The Christ with which we have to deal is not in any quantitative sense the Christ with which Jesus had to deal. But remember that Jesus said that to whom much is given, of him much will be required. Before we start envying the supreme capacity and vocation of Jesus, perhaps we should start remembering the supreme responsibility that accompanied that awe-

THE DIVINE THAT IS HUMAN

some capacity and vocation. Indeed, perhaps we had better look first at the haunting yet exciting responsibility which accompanies the capacity and the vocation large or small, which we ourselves do have. There are two temptations for any amateur trumpet player after hearing someone like a Raphael Mendez or an Al Hirt play the trumpet. One temptation is to go home and throw his or her trumpet away. But that is not the ultimate temptation. Inspired by one who is a master of the instrument, the ultimate temptation for any ordinary trumpet player is to go home and take out that old beat up horn and start practicing. It is to determine to do a better job than in the past, to play the greatest music which, under the circumstances and through the given capacity and vocation, can be produced.

Such inspiration is something to celebrate as we focus our gaze once again upon the boy child of Bethlehem who has become for Christians "Mr. Christ." His personification of the divine quality of life vividly confronts us with the tremendous Christ-power with which we individually and personally, here and now, have to deal.

6

THE STAR WE NEVER SAW BEFORE

When they [the wise men] saw the star, they rejoiced exceedingly with great joy.

Matthew 2:10

Tradition has it that almost every day the English weather bureau issues this forecast: "Rain, showers, fog, mist, disagreeable weather—bright intervals." It is much the same forecast God must have issued that first day of creation. Surely a crisp summary of the changeable climate of history to this date has been just that: "Rain, showers, fog, mist, disagreeable weather—bright intervals."

And the brightest interval of all in Christian history is the birth of Jesus into the world. "In him was life, and the life was the light of men." That light, far from being a flashing interval, has proved to be pervading radiance. "The light is still shining in the darkness, for the darkness has never put it out" (GOODSPEED). To this day Christ shows us stars we never saw before.

THE STAR WE NEVER SAW BEFORE

It is a good thing, too. For if his star was bright enough to pierce the darkness of his day, our day is dark enough to need the brightness of his star.

How acutely we need the light of his star to show us the God we never saw before:

> *The God who creates the majestic mountains but who cares for the falling sparrow;*
> *is wise beyond our meager understanding, yet understanding of our meager wisdom;*
> *requires moral perfection that is our despair but whose tender mercy is our good fortune.*
>
> *The God who is*
> *not an absentee landlord but a generous proprietor,*
> *not a despicable tyrant but a forgiving parent,*
> *not a neutral spectator but an active participant.*
>
> *The God who knows all about*
> *our cradles and our crosses,*
> *our shepherds and our kings,*
> *our Herod despots and our homeless refugees.*
>
> *A God who is so intimately related to human beings that the divine can be revealed to persons through persons.*

CHRISTMAS IS FOR CELEBRATING

*A God who not only gladly receives those who
with all their hearts truly seek,
but who also persistently seeks
those who have hardened
their hearts.*

The brilliant Jewish scholar Claude Montefiore set out to examine the Gospels to see what there was about the teaching of Jesus that might be distinctively new, something never before pronounced, or at least emphasized by any other Jewish prophet or rabbi. He singled out a figure which Jesus himself used: the picture of the Divine Shepherd going out after the lost sheep. Rabbi Montefiore said that this is a new figure, one of the "new excellences" of the Gospel. The kind of God Jesus discovered was a seeking God whose very nature it is to go the full distance into the wilderness in quest of lost creatures.

Does a God like that make any difference really? Well, black the star of a living, loving God out of a sky like ours and see what happens to your spirit. Remove insofar as you reasonably can, your faintest flicker of faith in a Creative Source which accounts for us, a Discernible Order which we encounter, and a Sustaining Grace to which we are accountable. Move through life for even an imaginary moment thinking of yourself not as a child of such a Creator but as a little, alienated orphan facing all your fears and

THE STAR WE NEVER SAW BEFORE

frustrations, your tragedies and your temptations, your dilemmas and your decisions. You find no more meaning in life than you put there. You discover no more resource for life than you produce there, and, stouthearted though you may be, do you not discover that your spirit shakes within you at the sheer horror and terror of such a thought?

After all, when the Source that accounts for us, the Order which we encounter, and the Grace to which we are accountable go, that is not all that goes:

> *The universe changes from our God's ordered world into matter without mind;*
> *History ceases to be God's story and becomes instead a tale told by two billion idiots;*
>
> *The human family degenerates from a caring community into a brood of swine jostling at a gigantic trough;*
> *The valley of the shadow of death changes from a pathway to God to a literal deadend street.*

It does make a difference:

> *When you cannot answer the meaning of your tragedy to believe that there is One who can;*
> *When you cannot lift yourself by your own broken bootstraps, to believe that there is One whose*

THE STAR WE NEVER SAW BEFORE

resources are available to you in a creative and responsible partnership.

It is just such a seeking and saving, caring and creating God whose Christmas star hangs in history's sky. And we had better not take that star for granted. For in a day like ours we need a God like that.

But the star of Christmas shines on in our darkness to show us the Man we never saw before. The occasion of Christmas is not the *birth* of Jesus. The occasion of Christmas is the birth of *Jesus!* We do more than celebrate a historical episode. We honor a persisting and identifiable person. He was very much like us in that he shared our human nature. He was very unlike us in the use he made of it:

He had no servants yet they called him Master.
He had no medicines yet they called him Healer.
He had no degrees yet they called him Teacher.

He had no armies yet kings feared him.
He had no toys yet children loved him.
He had no home yet disciples followed him.

He committed no crime yet they crucified him.
He won no victories yet he overcame the world.
He was buried in a tomb yet his presence persists
  with dynamic power.

CHRISTMAS IS FOR CELEBRATING

That is the Man whose star Christmas hangs in history's sky. Neither you nor I nor anyone else ever saw a Man like that until Jesus was born into the world.

But what can we do about a man like that? If you are not willing to put an exclamation mark after his name and stand at attention, then you must put a question mark after his name and sit in silence. If you do not follow him, the least you must do is to wonder about him. The one thing you cannot do is to ignore him. However unwitting our awareness of the impact of his life upon ours, the historical fact stands established that we are where we are today, doing what we are doing, in the way we are doing it, because once upon a time there lived a man named Jesus. Whatever our lives might have been without him, they are decisively different because of him. Even for those who are not committed to him, he is inextricably a part of the past that impinges upon the present of all who have lived ever since he lived.

But there is a principle which operates in the realm of ethical and spiritual values as in the arts. The more of a master you are in any realm the more respect you have for the true Master of that realm.

If you do not stand in awe of the Jesus whom Christmas celebrates, do not necessarily conclude that it marks you as smart. It may merely reveal

THE STAR WE NEVER SAW BEFORE

that you are flippant. There are really two basic attitudes that wise men and wise women of succeeding generations have taken toward him. Either they have followed him with respect, or they have wondered about him in silence. That is the kind of Man whose star Christmas hangs in history's sky. And we had better not take that star for granted. For in a day like this, we need a Man like that.

The light really begins to shine via the Christmas star once we begin to see not only the God we never saw before and the Man we never saw before, but when we begin to see the Selves we never saw before.

Bertrand Russell once described his reaction to watching apes in the zoo. When they were not performing gymnastic feats or cracking nuts, he thought he saw a strange, strained sadness in their eyes. He said one could almost imagine that they felt they ought to become more than they were, but could not discover the secret of how to do it. On the road of evolution they lost their way. Their cousins have moved on, and they have been left behind. He added that that type of strain and anguish seems to have entered the soul of civilized persons. We know there is something better than we have achieved almost within our grasp, yet we do not know where to seek it or how to find it.

That is strange, for persons no wiser than Bertrand Russell have known where to seek it—and what is more they have found it. "One man," says Emerson, "was true to what is in you and me." And still the light of his life shines on to show us this remarkable miracle: that what we ought to be is precisely what we potentially are. What God demands of us, God gives to us.

To this day, he wakes desires we never can forget. Whereas we have been preoccupied priests walking on the other side of suffering; he makes us eager to become Samaritans, stooping down to heal the hurts of the world. Whereas we have been prodigals trying to stifle the beyond within us with a pig-pen philosophy of life; he makes us yearn to become apostles of the values that really abide—justice and truth, goodwill and compassion. Whereas we have become harassed victims of a competitive economy, he makes us want to exemplify the poise and the peace that the world can never give, nor yet ever take away.

Once in the light of the Christmas star we have pondered and affirmed the best that there is in us, we can no longer settle for our pettiness; we are repelled by our selfishness. We want to grow away from our fragmentations toward wholeness, away from phoniness toward authenticity. Such is the image of the self Christmas hangs in our sky. And we must not take that star for granted. In a day like this, we need Selves like that.

What is the forecast for today and tomorrow?

CHRISTMAS IS FOR CELEBRATING

Black out of our skies the Christmas star of the God, the Man, and the Self we never saw before and the predictions may well be depressingly monotonous: "rain, showers, fog, mist, disagreeable weather." Restore the Christmas star to our sky and like the original Wise Men begin to steer by that star—then in, through, and beyond our personal and global darkness we shall celebrate—"bright intervals."

NOTES

1. Ralph W. Sockman, *The Higher Happiness* (Nashville: Abingdon-Cokesbury, 1950), p. 47.
2. Christopher Fry, "Christmas Faith."
3. Leslie D. Weatherhead, *Discipleship* (Nashville: Abingdon-Cokesbury, 1934), pp. 101-102.
4. J. Bronowski, *The Identity of Man* (Garden City, N.Y.: Natural History Press, 1965), pp. 10-11.
5. "A Tiny Egg" from pp. 209-210 in *More Children's Worship in the Church School* by Jeanette Perkins Brown.
6. Albert Schweitzer, *Out of My Life and Thought* (New York: Henry Holt, 1933), pp. 207-208.
7. J. Wallace Hamilton, *Serendipity* (Westwood, N.J.: Revell, 1965), p. 185.
8. William Temple, *Nature, Man and God* (London: Macmillan, 1960), p. 36.
9. Margery Williams, *The Velveteen Rabbit* (Garden City, N.Y.: Doubleday, 1958), pp. 16, 17. Used by permission.
10. Phillips Brooks, "O Little Town of Bethlehem."

CHRISTMAS IS FOR CELEBRATING

11. Phillips Brooks, "Christmas Carol."
12. Harold DeWolf, *A Theology of the Living Church* (New York: Harper & Brothers, 1953), p. 253.

Melvin E. Wheatley, Jr., received the A.B. degree from The American University, Washington, D.C., and the B.D. from Drew University, Madison, New Jersey. He has served various United Methodist Churches in California and Delaware and was elected Bishop by the Western Jurisdiction in 1972. He has taught at University of the Pacific, University of Southern California School of Religion, and Southern California School of Theology.

Bishop Wheatley is a frequent speaker on college campuses, at United Methodist annual conferences, and for community and interdenominational organizations. He has published numerous articles in religious and educational periodicals. Among his previously published books are *Going His Way, Our Man and the Church,* and *The Power of Worship.* Bishop Wheatley has served on the Board of Discipleship of The United Methodist Church and the Program Curriculum Committee of that Board. Presently he serves on the General Council on Ministries and the General Church Commission on the Status and Role of Women.